From Listings to Riches: A Craigslist Money Manual

Table of content

Chapter 1: Introduction

In the dynamic landscape of online commerce, Craigslist stands out as a powerful platform, offering a myriad of opportunities for individuals seeking to augment their income and entrepreneurial ventures. This chapter serves as a gateway to understanding the vast potential encapsulated within the virtual realms of Craigslist, exploring the multifaceted dimensions that make it an instrumental tool for those looking to make money in innovative ways.

We embark on this journey by delving into the very essence of Craigslist, dissecting its origins, and tracing the evolution that has shaped it into the digital marketplace behemoth it is today. From its humble beginnings in 1995 as an email distribution list to its current status as a global online marketplace covering diverse categories, Craigslist has become a virtual melting pot where buyers and sellers converge to exchange goods, services, and ideas.

As we navigate through the intricacies of Craigslist, we'll unravel the diverse range of categories and niches available, providing a panoramic view of the platform's expansive landscape. Understanding the unique characteristics of each category is crucial for anyone looking to capitalize on the immense potential that lies within specific markets. This chapter serves as a compass, guiding readers through the labyrinth of options and helping them identify the most promising avenues for their money-making endeavors.

Moreover, we explore the overarching principles that underpin successful ventures on Craigslist. From the art of crafting attention-grabbing headlines and descriptions to the strategic use of visuals that enhance product or service appeal, every detail contributes to the success of a listing. This chapter delves into the psychology of effective listings, offering insights into how sellers can optimize their presentations to attract the right audience and maximize their earning potential.

To set the stage for the chapters to come, we also touch on the broader context of online entrepreneurship and how Craigslist fits into the larger narrative of digital commerce. By understanding the historical context and the evolving nature of online marketplaces, readers can position themselves strategically to harness the full power of Craigslist in their pursuit of financial prosperity.

In essence, Chapter 1 serves as a comprehensive initiation into the world of making money on Craigslist. By the end of this chapter, readers will have gained a profound understanding of the platform's history, its diverse categories, and the fundamental principles that lay the groundwork for successful ventures. This knowledge will form the foundation upon which the subsequent chapters will build, equipping readers with the insights and perspectives necessary to navigate the intricate terrain of Craigslist with confidence and savvy.

Chapter 2: Navigating the Craigslist Landscape

As we embark on the journey of capitalizing on the vast potential Craigslist offers, Chapter 2 delves deep into the intricacies of navigating this dynamic online marketplace. By providing an in-depth exploration of the platform's functionalities, we equip readers with the essential knowledge needed to establish a strong presence and effectively engage in the myriad opportunities available.

The chapter commences with a detailed guide on the process of creating a Craigslist account and crafting a compelling profile. Understanding the nuances of profile creation is more than a mere formality; it is a strategic move that lays the groundwork for building trust and credibility within the Craigslist community. From selecting a profile picture that conveys professionalism to crafting a concise yet engaging bio, every element contributes to the initial impression users make on potential buyers or sellers.

Once the foundational elements are in place, we turn our attention to the expansive landscape of Craigslist's categories and niches.

By providing an extensive overview of the diverse range of sections available, readers gain insights into where their particular skills, interests, or inventory align with the demands of the market. From housing and jobs to services and goods, each category unfolds as a unique opportunity for users to explore and potentially monetize.

In addition to understanding the broad categories, Chapter 2 offers a nuanced examination of the subcategories and specialties that may often be overlooked. These hidden gems within Craigslist's labyrinth of options can present untapped opportunities for entrepreneurial ventures. By navigating through these subcategories, users can uncover niche markets that align with their expertise or passions, offering a strategic advantage in a competitive online environment.

To further enhance users' ability to navigate Craigslist effectively, the chapter provides insights into the search functionalities and filters available. Whether seeking specific items or scoping out the competition, mastering the search tools empowers users to streamline their Craigslist experience. Advanced search techniques and filters are explored, allowing readers to save time and energy while maximizing the relevance of their searches.

As we delve into the art of navigating Craigslist, the chapter also addresses the significance of understanding the platform's policies and guidelines. Comprehending the do's and don'ts ensures a smooth and compliant experience, mitigating the risk of potential pitfalls or account-related issues. By familiarizing themselves with Craigslist's terms of use, users can engage confidently and responsibly in the digital marketplace.

In summary, Chapter 2 serves as a comprehensive guide to navigating the Craigslist landscape. By understanding the nuances of account creation, profile optimization, category exploration, and search functionalities, readers are equipped with the tools needed to traverse the diverse terrain of Craigslist strategically. This knowledge lays the foundation for subsequent chapters, where we delve deeper into the specifics of maximizing earning potential within this dynamic online marketplace.

Chapter 3: Identifying Profitable Niches

As we venture further into the realm of leveraging Craigslist for financial gain, Chapter 3 unfolds as a comprehensive exploration into the art and science of identifying profitable niches. This crucial step is akin to unearthing hidden treasures within the expansive landscape of Craigslist, and it requires a nuanced understanding of market dynamics, consumer behavior, and emerging trends.

The chapter commences with an in-depth examination of high-demand categories, shedding light on the sectors where users can potentially find a lucrative intersection between supply and demand. By scrutinizing the data and metrics associated with these categories, readers gain insights into the pulse of the Craigslist marketplace, enabling them to make informed decisions about where to focus their entrepreneurial efforts.

Beyond the broader categories, the exploration extends to specific niches within each section. This involves a meticulous analysis of subcategories that may harbor untapped potential. By understanding the nuances of these specialized markets, users can position themselves as experts or enthusiasts in niche fields, thereby gaining a competitive edge and attracting a more targeted audience.

Moreover, Chapter 3 guides readers through the process of researching and identifying trends within their chosen niches. The dynamic nature of online marketplaces requires a keen eye for emerging patterns and evolving consumer preferences. Through thorough research methodologies and the utilization of analytical tools, users can stay ahead of the curve, positioning themselves strategically within burgeoning trends for sustained profitability.

In addition to quantitative analysis, the chapter delves into qualitative aspects of niche identification. This involves understanding the psychographics of the target audience—their preferences, pain points, and aspirations. By aligning offerings with the deeper needs and desires of Craigslist users, entrepreneurs can create listings that resonate on a personal level, fostering stronger connections and increasing the likelihood of successful transactions.

To facilitate the process of niche selection, Chapter 3 offers practical frameworks and exercises for readers to assess their own skills, interests, and resources. Through a self-discovery journey, users can pinpoint areas where their passion intersects with market demand, laying the foundation for a sustainable and fulfilling entrepreneurial venture.

Furthermore, the chapter explores the importance of adaptability in niche selection. The online marketplace is dynamic, and trends may shift over time. Readers are guided on how to continuously evaluate and reassess their chosen niches, ensuring that their offerings remain relevant and in-demand amid changing market dynamics.

In conclusion, Chapter 3 serves as an expansive guide to identifying profitable niches on Craigslist. Through a comprehensive exploration of high-demand categories, specific subcategories, trend analysis, psychographic considerations, and personal assessments, readers are equipped with the knowledge and tools needed to strategically position themselves within the diverse and ever-evolving landscape of Craigslist. This chapter lays the groundwork for the subsequent chapters, where we delve deeper into the practical strategies for capitalizing on the identified niches.

Chapter 4: Crafting Compelling Listings

Crafting compelling listings is an art form on Craigslist, and in Chapter 4, we embark on an extensive exploration of the intricacies involved in creating listings that not only capture attention but also drive engagement and conversions. As we delve into this crucial aspect of the money-making journey on Craigslist, readers will gain valuable insights into the psychology of effective listings and the strategic elements that contribute to their success.

The chapter begins with an in-depth analysis of the headline—the gateway to the listing. Readers will learn the subtle nuances of constructing headlines that are not only attention-grabbing but also succinctly convey the value proposition of the product or service. From the use of persuasive language to the inclusion of key details, every element of the headline is dissected to empower users in maximizing the visibility of their listings.

Moving beyond headlines, we explore the anatomy of persuasive descriptions. Crafting a compelling narrative around the product or service is a delicate balance between providing sufficient information and maintaining a sense of intrigue. This chapter guides users through the art of storytelling in listings, offering tips on how to create a narrative that resonates with potential buyers, emphasizing benefits, and addressing common pain points.

Visual appeal is a critical component of any successful Craigslist listing, and Chapter 4 delves into the strategic use of images. From selecting high-quality visuals that showcase the product from various angles to optimizing image sizes for faster loading, readers will discover practical techniques to enhance the overall visual impact of their listings. Additionally, we discuss the importance of honesty in visual representation to build trust with potential buyers.

An often-overlooked aspect of crafting listings is the implementation of keywords strategically. This chapter delves into the importance of keyword optimization for increased discoverability within Craigslist's search algorithms. Readers will learn how to conduct keyword research specific to their niche and integrate these terms seamlessly into their listings to improve visibility and attract a relevant audience.

The chapter further explores the role of pricing strategies in crafting compelling listings. From understanding competitive pricing to employing psychological pricing techniques, users gain insights into how to set prices that not only reflect the value of their offerings but also appeal to the target market. Strategies for effective negotiation are also discussed, providing users with the tools to navigate haggling scenarios successfully.

To add a personal touch to listings, Chapter 4 explores the concept of seller personas. Readers will discover how creating a relatable persona can humanize their listings, fostering a sense of connection with potential buyers. This approach goes beyond the transactional nature of online commerce, building trust and increasing the likelihood of successful transactions.

In summary, Chapter 4 serves as an expansive guide to crafting compelling listings on Craigslist. By dissecting the components of effective headlines, descriptions, images, keywords, pricing strategies, and the incorporation of seller personas, readers are equipped with the comprehensive knowledge needed to optimize their listings for maximum impact. This chapter sets the stage for the subsequent chapters, where we delve deeper into the intricacies of negotiation, building credibility, and scaling operations on Craigslist.

Chapter 5: Negotiation Strategies

Negotiation on Craigslist is a delicate dance that requires finesse, strategic thinking, and effective communication. In this expansive chapter, we delve into the multifaceted world of negotiation strategies, equipping readers with the tools and insights needed to navigate the often intricate and dynamic process of reaching mutually beneficial agreements.

The chapter begins by establishing a foundational understanding of effective communication in the context of online negotiations. Readers will explore the nuances of tone, language, and responsiveness, gaining insights into how to convey confidence and professionalism while building rapport with potential buyers or sellers. This forms the basis for establishing a positive and collaborative negotiation environment.

Understanding the psychological aspects of negotiation is crucial, and this chapter provides an in-depth exploration of the principles that govern successful negotiations on Craigslist. From the art of active listening to the utilization of empathy, readers will discover how to read between the lines, identify key motivations, and tailor their negotiation approach to the unique characteristics of each interaction.

To navigate the intricacies of setting prices and responding to offers, the chapter offers practical frameworks for readers to determine their negotiation boundaries. From determining the lowest acceptable price to recognizing when it's appropriate to stand firm, users will gain insights into how to navigate the delicate balance between securing a favorable deal and maintaining profitability.

Moreover, Chapter 5 explores the concept of value proposition in negotiations. Readers will learn how to articulate the unique value of their offerings and leverage this information strategically to justify pricing decisions. By aligning the perceived value with the listed price, users can enhance their negotiation position and increase the likelihood of reaching agreements that satisfy both parties.

As negotiations often extend beyond mere price discussions, the chapter also addresses the importance of compromise and finding common ground. Readers will discover how to identify mutually beneficial solutions, whether through adjustments in terms, bundled offerings, or other concessions that contribute to a positive and constructive negotiation process.

Recognizing and responding to different negotiation styles is a key element of successful interactions on Craigslist. This chapter provides an overview of various negotiation archetypes, offering readers insights into how to adapt their approach based on the characteristics of the counterparty. Whether facing a competitive negotiator or a collaborative problem-solver, understanding these styles empowers users to navigate diverse negotiation scenarios with confidence.

To further enrich the negotiation toolbox, the chapter explores the role of persuasion techniques. From storytelling to social proof, users will gain insights into how to influence perceptions and guide the negotiation process in their favor. This involves understanding the psychology of decision-making and tailoring communication strategies to appeal to the emotional and rational aspects of the negotiation counterpart.

In conclusion, Chapter 5 serves as a comprehensive guide to negotiation strategies on Craigslist. By exploring effective communication, psychological principles, price setting, value proposition, compromise, negotiation styles, and persuasive techniques, readers are equipped with a robust toolkit to navigate the diverse and nuanced landscape of online negotiations. This chapter lays the groundwork for subsequent chapters, where we delve deeper into building credibility, scaling operations, and addressing challenges within the Craigslist marketplace.

Chapter 6: Building Credibility on Craigslist

Building credibility on Craigslist is not merely about establishing trust; it's about cultivating a positive reputation that resonates within the online community. In this comprehensive chapter, we embark on a detailed exploration of the multifaceted strategies and practices that contribute to building and maintaining credibility on this dynamic platform.

The chapter commences with an examination of the foundational elements of credibility, emphasizing the importance of transparency and honesty in all interactions. Readers will discover how providing accurate and detailed information in listings sets the stage for trust, laying the groundwork for successful transactions and positive user experiences.

Establishing a positive reputation involves more than delivering a product or service—it extends to effective communication and responsiveness. This chapter delves into the art of timely and courteous communication, exploring how prompt responses to inquiries, acknowledgment of feedback, and clarity in transaction details contribute to the overall perception of reliability.

Moreover, we explore the concept of customer reviews and feedback on Craigslist. Readers will gain insights into the significance of reviews in shaping their online reputation and influencing the decisions of potential buyers or clients. Strategies for encouraging positive reviews and effectively addressing concerns or negative feedback are discussed, empowering users to actively manage their reputation on the platform.

Beyond individual transactions, building credibility involves consistent and ethical business practices. This chapter delves into the importance of delivering on promises, meeting or exceeding expectations, and resolving issues proactively. By fostering a commitment to customer satisfaction, users can position themselves as reliable and trustworthy entities within the Craigslist community.

The chapter also explores the role of personal branding on Craigslist. Readers will discover how creating a distinctive and memorable brand image contributes to their overall credibility. This involves aspects such as a recognizable profile picture, a consistent tone in communication, and a cohesive visual identity across listings. By crafting a brand that aligns with their values and resonates with their target audience, users can enhance their credibility and stand out in the competitive online marketplace.

Understanding the impact of ethical behavior on credibility, this chapter addresses potential pitfalls and challenges that users may encounter on Craigslist. From avoiding misleading practices to navigating disputes with professionalism, readers will gain insights into how ethical conduct not only safeguards their reputation but also contributes to the positive perception of the Craigslist community as a whole.

To enrich the discussion on building credibility, the chapter explores the concept of social proof. Readers will discover how leveraging testimonials, endorsements, and success stories can enhance their credibility by showcasing real-world examples of satisfied customers or clients. Strategies for collecting and showcasing social proof effectively are discussed, providing users with actionable steps to bolster their online reputation.

In conclusion, Chapter 6 serves as a comprehensive guide to building credibility on Craigslist. By exploring transparency, effective communication, customer reviews, ethical practices, personal branding, and the utilization of social proof, readers are equipped with a holistic understanding of the strategies that contribute to a positive online reputation. This chapter lays the foundation for subsequent chapters, where we delve deeper into scaling operations, advanced Craigslist techniques, and navigating legal considerations within the dynamic online marketplace.

Chapter 7: Scaling Your Operation

Scaling operations on Craigslist requires a strategic approach that goes beyond individual listings. In this expansive chapter, we embark on a detailed exploration of the multifaceted strategies and techniques that empower users to expand their reach, manage multiple listings efficiently, and ultimately grow their online ventures on this dynamic platform.

The chapter begins with an examination of the scalability mindset, emphasizing the importance of strategic planning and foresight. Readers will explore the concept of scalability as an ongoing process, understanding that successful growth on Craigslist involves anticipating challenges, optimizing workflows, and adapting to the evolving dynamics of the online marketplace.

Expanding reach and visibility is a key component of scaling operations, and this chapter delves into the various tools and features provided by Craigslist to enhance discoverability. From utilizing premium listings and featured posts to leveraging paid advertising options, users will gain insights into how to strategically invest in promoting their offerings for maximum impact.

Moreover, the chapter explores the concept of automation tools and techniques. As users navigate the challenges of managing multiple listings, streamlining repetitive tasks through automation becomes crucial. Readers will discover practical strategies for automating aspects of their Craigslist operations, saving time and resources while ensuring consistency and efficiency in their online endeavors.

Beyond automation, effective time management is paramount to scaling operations successfully. This chapter provides insights into creating efficient workflows, setting priorities, and managing time effectively to balance the demands of maintaining and expanding a growing Craigslist presence. Strategies for batching tasks, utilizing productivity tools, and delegating responsibilities are explored, empowering users to navigate the complexities of scaling.

As users aim to scale their operations, a nuanced understanding of analytics and data becomes increasingly important. This chapter delves into the role of data analysis in making informed decisions, identifying trends, and optimizing strategies for growth. Readers will explore key performance indicators (KPIs), tracking metrics relevant to their niche, and utilizing analytical tools to gain actionable insights.

To facilitate the process of managing multiple listings, readers will gain insights into effective organizational strategies. This involves categorizing listings, utilizing tags or labels, and employing tools within the Craigslist platform to maintain order and accessibility. By implementing systematic approaches to listing management, users can avoid overwhelm and streamline their operations for sustained growth.

In addition to managing listings, the chapter explores strategies for diversification within the Craigslist ecosystem. Readers will discover how exploring additional categories or expanding into complementary niches can contribute to a diversified and resilient online presence. Strategies for identifying opportunities for expansion and evaluating the feasibility of branching into new areas are discussed in detail.

To address the challenges associated with scaling, this chapter offers insights into maintaining quality control. From ensuring consistent customer service to monitoring the quality of products or services, users will discover strategies for upholding standards as they expand their operations. This involves establishing clear processes and guidelines to maintain the reputation and integrity of their Craigslist presence.

In conclusion, Chapter 7 serves as a comprehensive guide to scaling operations on Craigslist. By exploring the scalability mindset, expanding reach, leveraging automation, managing time effectively, analyzing data, organizing listings, diversifying offerings, and maintaining quality control, readers are equipped with a holistic understanding of the strategies that contribute to successful growth within the dynamic online marketplace. This chapter lays the foundation for subsequent chapters, where we delve deeper into advanced techniques, navigating challenges, and addressing legal considerations within the evolving landscape of Craigslist.

Chapter 8: Avoiding Scams and Pitfalls

Navigating the vast and diverse landscape of Craigslist, users must equip themselves with a comprehensive understanding of potential pitfalls and scams that can pose challenges to their online ventures. In this extensive chapter, we delve into the intricate nuances of recognizing and mitigating risks, ensuring a safe and secure experience within the dynamic Craigslist marketplace.

The chapter commences with an in-depth exploration of common scams prevalent on Craigslist. Readers will gain insights into various fraudulent schemes, including phishing attempts, counterfeit transactions, and misleading advertisements. Understanding the modus operandi of scammers is crucial for users to arm themselves with vigilance and make informed decisions in their interactions within the platform.

A pivotal aspect of avoiding scams involves recognizing red flags within listings and communications. This chapter provides readers with a detailed checklist of warning signs, empowering them to identify potentially fraudulent activities. From suspiciously low prices to requests for personal information, users will learn to scrutinize listings and messages for indicators that warrant caution.

Moreover, the chapter offers practical guidance on how to conduct due diligence when engaging in transactions on Craigslist. From researching the background of sellers or buyers to verifying the authenticity of products or services, readers will discover strategies for minimizing risks and making informed decisions that contribute to a secure and trustworthy online experience.

As users delve into the realm of in-person transactions, the chapter explores safety measures and best practices. Readers will gain insights into choosing secure locations for meetings, conducting transactions in well-lit and public spaces, and bringing a friend or notifying someone of their whereabouts during face-to-face exchanges. These precautions contribute to a safer and more secure transaction environment.

Educating oneself on Craigslist's own safety guidelines is paramount, and this chapter provides a comprehensive overview of the platform's recommended practices. Readers will gain insights into features such as anonymous email relay, which allows users to communicate without revealing personal email addresses, and other security measures implemented by Craigslist to protect its user base.

To further fortify their defenses against potential scams, readers will explore the importance of cybersecurity. This involves securing personal information, using strong and unique passwords, and being vigilant against phishing attempts. Understanding the digital landscape and implementing cybersecurity best practices contributes to a robust defense against online threats.

In addition to individual safety measures, the chapter delves into the significance of community awareness. Users will discover the value of reporting suspicious activities, scams, or potential fraud to Craigslist, contributing to the collective effort to maintain the integrity of the platform and protect fellow users from falling victim to scams.

Navigating potential pitfalls also involves understanding the legal aspects of transactions on Craigslist. This chapter provides an overview of legal considerations, such as contract formation, buyer and seller responsibilities, and the resolution of disputes. By gaining insights into the legal framework, users can navigate Craigslist transactions with a heightened awareness of their rights and obligations.

In conclusion, Chapter 8 serves as a comprehensive guide to avoiding scams and pitfalls on Craigslist. By exploring common scams, recognizing red flags, conducting due diligence, implementing safety measures, understanding Craigslist's safety guidelines, prioritizing cybersecurity, promoting community awareness, and considering legal aspects, readers are equipped with a holistic understanding of the strategies that contribute to a secure and trustworthy experience within the dynamic online marketplace. This chapter lays the foundation for subsequent chapters, where we delve deeper into advanced Craigslist techniques, legal and regulatory considerations, and emerging trends within the evolving landscape of online commerce.

Chapter 9: Advanced Craigslist Techniques

As users seek to elevate their Craigslist ventures to new heights, Chapter 9 delves into the realm of advanced techniques, providing an extensive exploration of strategies and practices that go beyond the basics. In this comprehensive chapter, readers will gain insights into sophisticated approaches that can further enhance their online presence, optimize their listings, and position themselves as adept entrepreneurs within the dynamic Craigslist marketplace.

The chapter commences with an in-depth examination of leveraging additional features within the Craigslist platform. From understanding the nuances of HTML in listings to utilizing premium features for enhanced visibility, readers will gain practical insights into maximizing the capabilities offered by Craigslist to create listings that stand out in a crowded marketplace.

Exploring the intricacies of A/B testing is a pivotal aspect of advanced techniques on Craigslist. This chapter provides readers with a comprehensive guide on how to conduct effective A/B tests to refine and optimize their listings. From experimenting with different headlines and descriptions to testing various images or pricing strategies, users can leverage data-driven insights to continuously improve the performance of their listings.

Moreover, the chapter delves into the concept of cross-promotion and collaboration within the Craigslist community. Readers will discover how forming strategic alliances with other users, businesses, or complementary services can broaden their reach and introduce their offerings to new audiences. Collaborative efforts, such as joint promotions or cross-listing agreements, can amplify visibility and contribute to mutually beneficial outcomes.

To enhance the visual appeal of listings, this chapter explores advanced techniques in photography and graphic design. Users will gain insights into professional-grade imagery, effective photo editing, and the strategic use of graphics or infographics within listings. Elevating the visual presentation of products or services can significantly impact buyer perception and engagement.

In addition to visuals, the chapter explores the role of storytelling and narrative-building in advanced Craigslist techniques. Readers will discover how crafting compelling narratives around their listings can evoke emotions, create connections with potential buyers, and differentiate their offerings in a meaningful way. The art of storytelling adds a layer of depth to listings, making them more memorable and impactful.

As users delve into the realm of advanced techniques, the chapter also addresses the importance of adapting strategies to evolving algorithms and trends. Readers will explore how staying abreast of changes within the Craigslist platform, such as updates to search algorithms or shifts in user behavior, can inform their approach to optimization and ensure continued relevance within the dynamic online marketplace.

Expanding beyond individual listings, the chapter discusses the potential of creating and managing multiple accounts strategically. Readers will gain insights into the considerations and best practices for managing multiple identities or storefronts on Craigslist, providing a nuanced approach to diversification and scale within the platform.

To optimize communication and customer engagement, the chapter explores advanced strategies for utilizing social media in conjunction with Craigslist. From integrating social media links within listings to leveraging social platforms for additional promotion and customer interaction, users will discover how to create synergies between their Craigslist presence and broader online networks.

In conclusion, Chapter 9 serves as a comprehensive guide to advanced Craigslist techniques. By exploring additional features, A/B testing, cross-promotion, photography and design, storytelling, adapting to trends, managing multiple accounts, and integrating social media, readers are equipped with a rich toolkit of strategies that can propel their Craigslist ventures to new heights. This chapter lays the foundation for subsequent chapters, where we delve into legal and regulatory considerations, emerging trends, and the future landscape of online commerce within the evolving Craigslist ecosystem.

Chapter 10: Real-Life Success Stories

In Chapter 10, we embark on a captivating journey through the narratives of real-life success stories within the realm of Craigslist entrepreneurship. This extensive chapter offers a collection of interviews, case studies, and firsthand accounts that provide readers with valuable insights into the diverse experiences of individuals who have navigated the Craigslist landscape, overcome challenges, and achieved remarkable success in their online ventures.

The chapter commences with an exploration of the varied paths that led entrepreneurs to discover and harness the potential of Craigslist. Through interviews with successful Craigslist users, readers will gain a deep understanding of the motivations, aspirations, and initial challenges faced by these individuals as they embarked on their journeys toward financial prosperity on the platform.

As we delve into the narratives of these Craigslist entrepreneurs, the chapter unfolds with diverse case studies that showcase the unique strategies, innovative approaches, and lessons learned from their experiences. From individuals who transformed a side hustle into a full-time business to those who successfully navigated niche markets, each case study offers a nuanced perspective on the multifaceted nature of success on Craigslist.

Readers will be treated to insights into the evolution of these success stories over time. Understanding the milestones, setbacks, and pivotal moments within the entrepreneurial journeys provides a realistic and relatable view of the challenges and triumphs inherent in building a thriving presence on Craigslist. These stories serve as inspiration and practical guidance for readers seeking to carve their paths in the online marketplace.

Moreover, the chapter explores the role of adaptability and resilience in the face of adversity. Through candid discussions with successful entrepreneurs who navigated challenges such as market fluctuations, competition, or external factors, readers will gain valuable insights into the mindset and strategies that contributed to overcoming obstacles and turning setbacks into opportunities.

To enrich the narrative, the chapter delves into the strategies and tactics employed by these successful individuals to maximize their earnings on Craigslist. From the specifics of effective listings and negotiation techniques to scaling operations and building a brand, readers will gain practical takeaways and actionable advice based on the real-world experiences of those who have successfully navigated the Craigslist landscape.

The chapter also highlights the importance of community and networking in the journey to success on Craigslist. Entrepreneurs often find support, insights, and collaboration opportunities within the Craigslist community. Through the experiences shared in this chapter, readers will discover how fostering connections, participating in forums, and engaging with fellow users can contribute to a richer and more rewarding entrepreneurial experience.

In addition to individual success stories, the chapter explores collective achievements within niche markets. By examining case studies of entrepreneurs who identified and capitalized on specific trends or opportunities within Craigslist, readers will gain insights into the strategic thinking and market awareness that contributed to their achievements.

As we delve into the diverse and inspiring tales of Craigslist success, the chapter concludes with reflections on the overarching principles that unite these narratives. Themes such as perseverance, customer-centric approaches, continuous learning, and the adaptability to change emerge as key pillars that support sustainable and fulfilling entrepreneurial journeys on Craigslist.

In conclusion, Chapter 10 serves as a captivating exploration of real-life success stories within the Craigslist ecosystem. Through interviews, case studies, and firsthand accounts, readers gain a deep understanding of the motivations, strategies, challenges, and triumphs experienced by individuals who have carved their paths to success on the platform. This chapter stands as a source of inspiration and practical guidance for readers seeking to embark on their own journeys within the dynamic world of Craigslist entrepreneurship.

Chapter 11: Legal and Regulatory Considerations

As entrepreneurs navigate the dynamic landscape of Craigslist, a comprehensive understanding of the legal and regulatory aspects becomes paramount. In this extensive chapter, we embark on a detailed exploration of the legal considerations that underpin online commerce on Craigslist, providing readers with the knowledge and insights necessary to operate within the bounds of the law and mitigate potential risks.

The chapter commences with an overview of the legal framework governing transactions on Craigslist. Readers will gain insights into the general principles of contract law that underlie the agreements formed through Craigslist interactions. Understanding the elements of a legally binding contract, including offer, acceptance, and consideration, serves as a foundational understanding for entrepreneurs engaging in online transactions.

To enhance this understanding, the chapter delves into the importance of clear and transparent communication within Craigslist transactions. Users will discover how the details provided in listings, negotiations, and agreements contribute to the formation of legally binding contracts. Clarity in communication not only facilitates smoother transactions but also mitigates the risk of disputes arising from misunderstandings.

Moreover, the chapter explores legal considerations related to consumer protection. Understanding the rights and responsibilities of buyers and sellers is crucial for ensuring compliance with consumer protection laws. Topics such as accurate product descriptions, fair pricing, and the disclosure of relevant information contribute to ethical and legally sound transactions on Craigslist.

As users engage in transactions involving tangible goods, the chapter addresses legal considerations related to product liability. Readers will gain insights into their responsibilities regarding the safety and quality of the products they sell, as well as the potential legal ramifications of selling defective or harmful items. Strategies for mitigating product liability risks are discussed to empower entrepreneurs to prioritize consumer safety.

The chapter also provides an in-depth examination of online privacy considerations within the Craigslist ecosystem. Users will explore the importance of safeguarding personal information, understanding Craigslist's privacy policies, and adopting best practices to protect their own privacy and that of their customers. Privacy compliance contributes to the establishment of a secure and trustworthy online environment.

In addition to legal considerations within individual transactions, the chapter explores the implications of intellectual property laws on Craigslist. Users will gain insights into copyright, trademark, and patent considerations related to listings, images, and brand identities. Understanding how to respect and protect intellectual property rights contributes to ethical conduct and legal compliance within the online marketplace.

As the digital landscape continues to evolve, the chapter addresses emerging legal issues and trends relevant to Craigslist entrepreneurs. This includes considerations related to emerging technologies, data protection regulations, and changes in consumer behavior that may impact legal frameworks and require continuous adaptation from entrepreneurs.

To further enrich the legal toolkit, the chapter explores dispute resolution mechanisms within the Craigslist platform. Users will gain insights into options for resolving conflicts, including negotiation, mediation, and the legal recourse available in cases of serious disputes. Understanding these mechanisms empowers entrepreneurs to navigate challenges effectively and seek resolution in a fair and efficient manner.

Moreover, the chapter provides guidance on the importance of keeping accurate records of transactions. Maintaining documentation, including communication logs, transaction details, and any agreements made, serves as a crucial resource in the event of disputes or legal inquiries. The practice of record-keeping contributes to transparency and accountability within Craigslist transactions.

In conclusion, Chapter 11 serves as a comprehensive guide to legal and regulatory considerations within the Craigslist ecosystem. By exploring contract law principles, consumer protection, product liability, online privacy, intellectual property, emerging legal issues, dispute resolution mechanisms, and the importance of record-keeping, readers are equipped with a holistic understanding of the legal landscape that underpins their online ventures. This chapter lays the foundation for subsequent chapters, where we delve into emerging trends, future considerations, and the evolving dynamics of online commerce within the Craigslist platform.

Chapter 12: Emerging Trends and Future Considerations

In Chapter 12, we embark on a forward-looking exploration of emerging trends and future considerations within the dynamic landscape of Craigslist. This extensive chapter provides readers with a visionary perspective, offering insights into the evolving dynamics of online commerce and how entrepreneurs can position themselves to thrive amidst technological advancements, shifting consumer behaviors, and the continuous evolution of the digital marketplace.

The chapter commences with an examination of the role of technology in shaping the future of Craigslist entrepreneurship. Readers will gain insights into emerging technologies, such as artificial intelligence (AI), augmented reality (AR), and blockchain, and how these innovations may impact the user experience, listings optimization, and transaction security on the platform. Understanding the potential applications of these technologies positions entrepreneurs to stay ahead of the curve and harness new tools for business growth.

As the world becomes increasingly interconnected, the chapter explores the significance of globalization within the Craigslist ecosystem. Readers will gain insights into the opportunities and challenges presented by a global audience, understanding how entrepreneurs can strategically expand their reach beyond local markets and engage with diverse consumer bases. Exploring strategies for cross-border transactions and navigating international regulations positions users to tap into the global potential of Craigslist.

Moreover, the chapter delves into the evolving landscape of consumer behavior and expectations. Readers will explore how changing demographics, preferences, and societal shifts influence the way users interact with online marketplaces. Adapting to these shifts requires a nuanced understanding of emerging consumer trends and a willingness to innovate in response to evolving expectations.

To enrich the discussion, the chapter explores the intersection of sustainability and entrepreneurship on Craigslist. Readers will gain insights into the growing importance of eco-friendly practices, ethical sourcing, and sustainable business models within the online marketplace. Understanding how sustainability aligns with consumer values and preferences allows entrepreneurs to cultivate a socially responsible presence on Craigslist.

As users navigate the ever-changing digital landscape, the chapter addresses the impact of data privacy regulations on Craigslist entrepreneurship. Readers will gain insights into evolving data protection laws and how compliance with these regulations is becoming increasingly crucial. Strategies for safeguarding user information, ensuring consent, and navigating the complexities of data privacy contribute to ethical and legally sound business practices.

The chapter also delves into the evolving role of social media and influencer marketing within the Craigslist ecosystem. Readers will explore how entrepreneurs can leverage social platforms to complement their Craigslist presence, build brand awareness, and engage with their target audience. Understanding the synergies between social media and online marketplaces provides users with additional channels for promotion and customer interaction.

Moreover, the chapter explores the impact of user-generated content and community engagement on the future of Craigslist entrepreneurship. Readers will gain insights into how user reviews, community forums, and collaborative initiatives contribute to the vibrancy and trustworthiness of the Craigslist community. Strategies for fostering community engagement and leveraging user-generated content position entrepreneurs to build stronger connections with their audience.

In addition to technological and consumer-centric trends, the chapter addresses the potential regulatory landscape of online marketplaces. Readers will gain insights into how legislative changes may impact the operation of Craigslist and other online platforms. Understanding regulatory considerations positions entrepreneurs to adapt their strategies and operations to comply with evolving legal frameworks.

To navigate the future landscape of Craigslist entrepreneurship, the chapter explores the concept of continuous learning and adaptability. Readers will discover the importance of staying informed about industry trends, technological advancements, and changes within the Craigslist platform. A commitment to ongoing learning and adaptability allows entrepreneurs to pivot, innovate, and seize emerging opportunities within the dynamic online marketplace.

In conclusion, Chapter 12 serves as a visionary exploration of emerging trends and future considerations within the Craigslist ecosystem. By examining the role of technology, globalization, changing consumer behaviors, sustainability, data privacy, social media, community engagement, regulatory landscapes, and the importance of continuous learning, readers are equipped with insights that go beyond the present moment. This chapter not only provides a roadmap for navigating the evolving dynamics of online commerce but also serves as an invitation for entrepreneurs to embrace innovation and position themselves as leaders within the future landscape of Craigslist entrepreneurship.

Conclusion

As we draw the curtains on this comprehensive guide to Craigslist entrepreneurship, we reflect on the expansive journey we've taken through the intricacies of this dynamic online marketplace. From the foundational principles of leveraging Craigslist for financial gain to the advanced techniques, legal considerations, and future trends that shape the evolving landscape, this guide has aimed to equip readers with a holistic understanding of the multifaceted world of Craigslist entrepreneurship.

At its core, Craigslist offers a digital canvas where entrepreneurial aspirations can take shape, providing a platform where users can connect, transact, and build communities. The journey began with the exploration of fundamental concepts, such as understanding the Craigslist marketplace, creating compelling listings, and mastering the art of negotiation. As users progressed through the chapters, the guide unfolded into an expansive repository of knowledge, offering nuanced insights into niche identification, credibility building, and scaling operations.

The narrative delved into the psychological intricacies of effective communication, the art of crafting listings that resonate, and the strategies for negotiating win-win agreements. From the nuances of pricing strategies to the importance of building a credible online presence, readers were guided through a comprehensive exploration of the skills and tactics that contribute to success on Craigslist.

The guide then transitioned into the realm of advanced techniques, offering readers a glimpse into the sophisticated strategies employed by successful entrepreneurs. A/B testing, cross-promotion, visual storytelling, and the integration of social media emerged as tools in the entrepreneurial toolkit, providing users with the means to elevate their Craigslist ventures to new heights.

Legal and regulatory considerations took center stage in a detailed exploration of the contractual foundations of transactions, consumer protection, and the implications of product liability. The guide underscored the importance of ethical conduct, privacy considerations, and navigating the legal landscape to ensure that Craigslist entrepreneurs operate within the bounds of the law and build a foundation of trust with their clientele.

As we delved into the rich tapestry of real-life success stories, readers were treated to inspiring accounts of individuals who navigated challenges, embraced innovation, and carved their paths to financial success on Craigslist. These stories served as beacons of inspiration, illustrating the diverse ways in which entrepreneurial journeys unfold within the dynamic and ever-evolving ecosystem of Craigslist.

The guide then cast its gaze into the future, exploring emerging trends and future considerations that will shape the trajectory of Craigslist entrepreneurship. From the integration of advanced technologies to the globalization of online markets, sustainability initiatives, and the evolving role of social media, readers gained foresight into the trends that will define the future landscape of Craigslist entrepreneurship.

In conclusion, this guide is not merely a collection of words on digital pages; it is an invitation for entrepreneurs to embark on a journey of exploration, innovation, and continuous learning within the expansive realm of Craigslist. It is a testament to the potential that lies within the digital marketplace and the opportunities that await those who approach entrepreneurship with a blend of strategic thinking, adaptability, and a commitment to ethical conduct.

As we bid farewell to these pages, we encourage readers to embrace the knowledge gained and embark on their Craigslist journeys with confidence. Whether you're a budding entrepreneur, an experienced business owner, or someone contemplating the possibilities that Craigslist offers, the principles and insights shared in this guide are designed to serve as a compass on your path to success.

May your Craigslist ventures be marked by resilience in the face of challenges, innovation in your strategies, and a commitment to building not just profitable enterprises but also thriving communities within the digital landscape. As the Craigslist ecosystem continues to evolve, so too does the potential for entrepreneurial success. Here's to the journey ahead, filled with possibilities, growth, and the fulfillment of your entrepreneurial aspirations within the dynamic and ever-expanding world of Craigslist.